The Well
and
The Cathedral

An Entrance Meditation

BOOKS BY IRA PROGOFF

At A Journal Workshop: The Basic Text and Guide for Using the Intensive Journal Process, 1975

Life Study: Experiencing Creative Lives by the *Intensive Journal* Method, 1983

The Practice of Process Meditation: The *Intensive Journal* Way to Spiritual Experience, 1980

The Symbolic and the Real, 1963

Depth Psychology and Modern Man, 1959

The Death and Rebirth of Psychology, 1956

The Cloud of Unknowing, 1957

The Image of an Oracle, 1964

Jung's Psychology and Its Social Meaning, 1953

Jung, Synchronicity and Human Destiny, 1973

The Star/Cross, 1971

The White Robed Monk, 1972

The Well and The Cathedral, 1971, 1977

The Well
and
The Cathedral

An Entrance Meditation

Ira Progoff

DIALOGUE HOUSE LIBRARY/NEW YORK

Published by Dialogue House Library
80 East 11 Street, New York, New York 10003
Copyright © 1972, 1977 by Ira Progoff
First Printing, 1971
Second Printing, 1972
Second Enlarged Edition, 1977

Library of Congress Cataloging in Publication Data

1. Meditations.   I   *The Well and the Cathedral*
BV4832.2P75   1976   2481.3   76-20823
ISBN 87941-004-3   Paperback ISBN 87941-005-01

Printed in the United States of America

THIRD REVISED EDITION 1983

Dedicated to

Matt Roberts

1925-1976

Designer of the Intensive Journal Logo,
he had almost completed designing
this book when he was called away.

A friend beyond guile.

Table of Contents

Preface to the Entrance Meditation Series / **15**

The Well and the Cathedral

I   Muddy/Clear: The Mirror of the Water / 33

II   Feeling the Movement of Life / 45

III   The Center Point Within Me / 59

IV   Into the Well of the Self / 73

V   The Downward/Upward Journey / 87

VI   The Waters Beyond the Well / 101

VII   Sharing the Underground Stream / 117

VIII   Entering the Cathedral / 133

Perspectives

1. From the Anonymous Monk to the Modern Person / 151

2. The Unitary Connection / 161

THE ENTRANCE MEDITATION SERIES

The Well and the Cathedral
The Star/Cross
The White Robed Monk

Preface

to the

Entrance

Meditation

Series

The meditations in this series have evolved in the course of a decade of use in public workshops, in religious services, in university teaching and in therapeutic work. Their purpose is to provide a means of *entering* the realm of quiet and depth where interior knowing takes place.

Where a person's spiritual life is concerned, we know that the door opens inward. It is through this door that we gain access to the elusive range of awarenesses where we find the meaning of our lives. Entrance Meditation enables us to go to that place within ourselves from which we can reach beyond ourselves. This is its purpose. Once Entrance Meditation has taken us through the entry way, it leaves us free to follow our own rhythms of inner experience and to move in whatever direction to explore whatever doctrines feel right to us.

Some of us may then embark on a great voyage of inward exploration and discovery, finding new realities we never perceived before. Others of us will remain within traditions and beliefs that we have always known, but our Entrance Meditation experience will so deepen our perception of their meaning that we will feel we have just discovered an altogether new truth. There are many paths that can be followed once we are within the realm of spiritual experience. We have true inner religious freedom there. The purpose of these meditations is to enable us to enter that realm. Our entrance meditations thus become the base and neutral starting point for all the further spiritual recognitions that may come to us. By providing a non-doctrinal means of gaining access to our inner space, they enable us to perceive and judge for ourselves the quality and the reality of the spiritual dimension of experience.

The conception of entrance meditation was originally developed within the framework of the *Intensive Journal* program. Over the years the meditations included in this series have had their largest use as aids for deepening personal experience within the context of *Intensive Journal* workshops. But the use of these entrance meditations is by no means limited to *Intensive Journal* work. They have been used independently by ministers conducting meditative services, by philosophy professors seeking to take their students to the inner place where they can share the experiences of the great philosophers of history, and by therapists of various types seeking to establish a depth atmosphere for their patients or clients.

The reports that have been brought to me regarding these experiences indicate that the use of entrance meditation is especially valuable in situations where a deepening of atmosphere facilitates the work that has been undertaken, whatever the purposes or beliefs of that work may be. One important reason it is able to do this is that these meditations tend to establish an atmosphere by means of symbols that are altogether neutral. These symbols are not tied to any specific system of doctrine or belief, and yet they express fundamental truths of human existence. They provide a vehicle, a means of entering the deep realms of reality in human experience. Thus they can serve in a neutral, non-dogmatic fashion as a way inward. And each person can reach by means of them a contact with truth in the terms of his or her own traditions and consciousness.

These meditations arose from experiences that came to me over a period of time in the course of my personal work in the *Intensive Journal* process, and especially in my personal practice of Process Meditation. Originally they were intended merely to give expression to my personal experiences. As I used them in *Intensive Journal* workshops, however, and then as others used them in their own frameworks wherever a deepened atmosphere might be helpful, we found that these experiences served a more-than-personal use. With this thought in mind they have been worked with experimentally over the years, and published in various editions on a trial and error basis in search of the format in which they can best serve.

The present edition of the Entrance Meditation Series is the result of this decade-long process of experimentation. It now contains *The Well and the Cathedral, The White Robed Monk,* and *The Star/ Cross* in a unified format, each moving through a cycle of eight units of meditative experience. Each unit is self-contained so that it can be used individually but the eight units in each of the volumes move in sequence developing their theme through a full cycle of experiences. When you work with these entrance meditation books, you may find that you prefer to work with each volume as a whole. Or you may find that you prefer to choose particular sections of the individual volumes and concentrate on them, using them to deepen and open your own experience. Work experimentally with them until you find the way that is spiritually most valuable for you.

Of the three volumes in this series *The Well and the Cathedral* expresses in the most fundamental form the principles that underlie the cycles of meditative experience. It contains a minimum of symbols, and these are mainly metaphors chosen for their functional use in helping a person move inward. The symbols serve as vehicles by which we can enter the depth levels of experience. They take you immediately into the practice of entrance meditation so that you can know it directly by experiencing it. And you experience it by participating in its practice.

In order to begin, there is little need to elaborate the principles and methods of entrance meditation. Essentially you can begin to use these meditations in the same way that a fish learns to swim: it finds itself in the water and it does what comes naturally. In the same natural way you can move directly into your meditative experience starting with any one of the volumes in this series. After your work in the quiet way of entrance meditation has established a deep atmosphere in which you can move about comfortably, you may wish to continue with the active procedures of Process Meditation. But that is a further step and an option before you.*

As you work with *The Well and the Cathedral* you will perceive that its neutral symbols take you inward, and then draw you back up to the surface of

* For the principles and techniques of Process Meditation see Ira Progoff, *The Practice of Process Meditation*, Dialogue House Library, N.Y. 1980. This is a companion volume to Ira Progoff, *At a Journal Workshop*, the basic guide and text of the *Intensive Journal* process (1975 cloth, 1977 paperback).

life. It is a cyclical movement. But it is also progressive because each phase of the cycle tends to take you deeper than the one before. There is thus a cumulative, deepening effect that establishes itself as you continue with the sequence of units of *The Well and the Cathedral*. But nothing of what takes place determines or even suggests what your experiences will be or what aspects of truth you will recognize. It merely gives you a progressive means of entering the depth dimension of your inner life.

There are many theories that deal with this inner realm, seeking to tell us what it is and what it contains. Many philosophies in the course of history have spoken of its mysteries, claiming to describe what is to be found there, giving a roadmap and instructions, telling seekers how they should behave. Entrance meditation makes no such presumption, but its practice does open another possibility. It enables us actually to enter our own inner space in order that we can find out for ourselves what is there. It does not predetermine what we shall discover. It does not give us rules telling us how we *should* experience it, nor what we shall believe about what we find there. It simply takes us to a progressively deeper place in quietness and then lets us go free, each to perceive a larger dimension of reality in which we may place the meaning of our life.

Each of the sequences of entrance meditation in this series follows the procedure of taking us progressively inward into the depths and then letting us go free to explore. The eight units of *The Well and the Cathedral* express this essence of entrance meditation in an altogether non-doctrinal form. The experiences described there are generic and universal. The experiences described in *The Star/Cross* and *The White Robed Monk* are more specific and individualized. Their symbols tend to set a direction and establish a definite tone for the inner work that is done with them. The experiences of *The White Robed Monk* move in a contemplative direction, invoking the atmosphere that comes with systematic religious practice. They do not presume any specific religious discipline, however. The experiences of *The Star/Cross* draw upon the spirituality of the world of nature, taking us each "into the forest of our life." There we come to the further questions of social justice and the painful events of history, seeking to understand them by the light of inner vision, "the path of the Prophets of old." Each of us may then consider the problems of society and history in our own spiritual perspective.

As we work in them, we must bear in mind that all three sequences of entrance meditation are only starters. They take us inward; and after they have taken us through the doorway into the depth dimension of experience, they give us the freedom to continue on our own. At any given time we may find that the particular cycle of meditation with which we are working is shaping our experiences, perhaps by influencing at a non-conscious level the direction in which we move, perhaps by the suggestive quality of its symbols. Each of us can then choose which cycles of entrance meditation we shall work with most actively. We may find also that there are certain units within the entrance meditations that we feel to be more closely related to our inner condition, more akin to our spiritual needs at the time.

There are a few specific guidelines that will be helpful in working with the entrance meditations in this series.

Our first step is to read a unit of meditation to ourselves, or to hear it read at a meditation workshop or service, or to play it on a cassette. We should continue with it until we come to the cue phrase at the close of the unit, "In the Silence . . . In the Silence." It is best to continue with it through the full reading of the unit, and not to leave it in the middle, not even in order to record a fresh stirring of experience. We wish to allow the cyclical movement of each unit to draw us fully into the stillness. If new experiences stir within us, we can let them accumulate and still remember them, recording them briefly as we come into the silence. In the midst of the meditation we do not think about it nor evaluate it nor interpret it. We simply enter the meditation, become part of it and go with it without seeking to direct or shape it in any way.

While reading or listening to the meditation, we consciously breathe slowly and softly. We do not follow any special or complicated calisthenic of breathing. We simply breathe in our accustomed way as feels natural to us. Now, however, as we are sitting in stillness, we breathe a little more slowly than we ordinarily would. First we establish the rhythm that feels right to us, and then we try to continue it in a regular way, remaining loose and relaxed as we do so.

Sustaining the breathing in a comfortable and steady rhythm is an important step in beginning the process of meditation. As we proceed and become more accustomed to it, we let ourselves go a little slower and a little slower. Bit by bit in our time of quietness, our breathing slows its pace. As it does so, our entire being, our thinking, our feeling, the tempo of our consciousness and our life, slows its pace. It is a time when the muddiness of our existence can settle into stillness and begin to clarify itself.

In working with a text of entrance meditation, it

is best to proceed one unit at a time, allowing ample time for silence after each unit of meditation. Each unit closes with the phrase, "In the Silence . . . In the Silence" and this is the cue for each of us to move into our own silence. Eyes closed, we turn our attention inward. We are looking inward, but we are not looking merely for things that can be seen. We are looking inward for sounds and words, for symbols and intuitions, for direct knowings and sensations of every kind that may come to us when our attention is turned to the large Twilight realm of Self that lies between unconscious sleep and waking consciousness.* In this state we do not seek any particular type of perception. We do not preconceive what our experience is to be, and especially we do not seek to direct it along any predetermined channel.

When we go into our silence and move into the Twilight range of experience, we are truly exploring. We are looking for information and guidance from a quality of consciousness within us that is other than the thoughts of our personal mind. We try to avoid intruding our expectations and ideas as

* For a discussion of Twilight Imaging and other related aspects of the *Intensive Journal* method, see Ira Progoff, *At a Journal Workshop*, Chapter 6, pp. 77ff., Dialogue House Library, N.Y., 1975. See also, Progoff, *The Practice of Process Meditation*, Chapters 5-9.

to what our experience "should" or will be. In particular, we try to refrain from intruding our desires or our willful directions as to what we "want" our experience to be. We are trying to draw new awarenesses from the transpersonal wisdom of life that is carried in the depths within us beyond our egos. One purpose of our practice of entrance meditation is to enable us to learn gradually how to do this. We practice letting it come as it comes, while we remain altogether open and receptive.

In the practice of entrance meditation we are observers of whatever is taking place within us as we sit in silence with our eyes closed and our attention turned inward. What we observe may be visual images that we see, words spoken, themes of music that we hear, sensations within our body, direct intuitive knowings. Whatever its form, as we perceive it we take cognizance of it. We do not judge it, but we recognize it. Neutrally, non-judgmentally, we accept its existence. We accept each perception on the Twilight level as it is, as a fact of our inner process and of our observation. We take note of it and we record it without evaluation.

As new experiences and perceptions come to us, it becomes essential that we record the inner events that are taking place. We should allow sufficient time for our free inner movement to build its own atmosphere and momentum. But we should not let so much time pass that we accumulate more perceptions than we can hold in our memory. On the one hand we do not wish to disrupt the flow of our inner experience. On the other hand we know that if we do not record our experiences as they are happening we shall very likely forget them. And then it will be virtually impossible to recall them again. The key lies in maintaining a balance, a rhythm between the inner perception and the outer recording. It is a rhythm to which we gradually become attuned.

The best way to proceed seems to be to learn to go back and forth from the inner to the outer levels, and back inward again.* In time we become accustomed to making quick, brief but adequate, entries. Writing them from the deep place with our eyes only slightly open, these entries will often be only barely legible when we seek to read them back to ourselves. If, however, we return to rewrite them without letting too long a period elapse, the inner events will be fresh enough in our minds so that we can transcribe and enlarge the notes, even with only a few barely legible words to guide us. Afterwards we take as much time as we need to describe in

* See, e.g., *The Well and the Cathedral*, Unit V, The Downward/Upward Journey.

detail all that has taken place, amplifying the nuances and elaborating any points that may stimulate us further when we read them back weeks or even months in the future.

An important part of this edition is the open space on the pages on the left side of the book. Those empty pages are for your spontaneous Meditation Log entries. We record what takes place within us as we explore and have new experiences on the Twilight level in the course of our entrance meditations. In what we write here we make no interpretations, nor do we elaborate or explain. We simply describe, briefly and directly, the elusive and subjective perceptions, images and emotions that arise in us in the course of our meditations. And then we move on. It is important also that we record the date of each entry. That will be a valuable piece of information for us when we return to the Meditation Log at a later time.

If you are already working with the *Intensive Journal* process you may wish to record your experiences directly in the Meditation Log section of the *Intensive Journal* workbook that you are using. That will save a step. But a number of persons have told me they feel they have benefited greatly by using the Meditation Log pages in the earlier printings of these entrance meditations. They have used the

Meditation Log in these printed volumes as a means of retaining the spontaneous experiences that came to them while they were working with the text, later copying their entries into the larger Meditation Log section in their *Intensive Journal* workbook. There is a particular value in using the Meditation Log pages in this edition to catch and record your experiences as they come to you while you are in the midst of your work. It is apparently an experience that is common to many persons to find that in the course of copying the entries to transfer them from one book to the other a great deal more is stimulated. Additional experiences are evoked. The recording and transcription of our inner experiences thus become an integral part of the progressive extension of consciousness that is the goal of our entrance meditation work.

Those who are already working in the *Intensive Journal* program are familiar with the varied measures available to us for drawing our Meditation Log entries into an expanding spiritual process. They know that in the *Intensive Journal* work the Meditation Log is not merely a passive recording instrument like a diary; it serves an active, energy-building function. After collecting the raw materials of our inner lives, the Meditation Log selectively feeds the data into the appropriate sections of the

Intensive Journal workbook. Here this material combines with other relevant images and thoughts recorded in other sections and together they may move through a varied combination of exercises. All of these are active exercises, evocation of both psyche and spirit, that build energy and movement as they generate new inner experiences. In the course of these exercises and experiences a person's varied beliefs and religious concerns, intimations and wonderings about meaning in life, are often stimulated and extended into a progressive, open-minded reaching toward truth.

In this phase of the work we are finally able to draw upon the full range of possibilities that the *Intensive Journal* method makes available to us. After using the basic *Intensive Journal* techniques to set the perspective of our life history and to clarify our personal relationships, we can proceed to the more-than-personal issues, the large spiritual agenda of Process Meditation. It is this further phase of the meditative discipline that enables us to expand our spiritual awareness with inner experiences that are directly related to the actualities, the goals and meanings, of our everyday life.*

* For the various ways of working with the Meditation Log section in the *Intensive Journal* workbook, see, in particular, *The Practice of Process Meditation*, Chapters 5, 6, 7, 8, 17, 18.

This is the point of transition in our meditative work. Here we take the important step from the fundamental introductory exercises of entrance meditation to the broad range of explorations and ongoing spiritual involvements that open to us with the practice of Process Meditation. By means of our entrance meditation experiences we can enter the dimension of spiritual reality where inner experiences and transpersonal awareness can come to us. We record these in our Meditation Log. These collected entries then become the raw spiritual data that serve as base points from which we launch our active inner explorations using the Process Meditation techniques within the *Intensive Journal* method. It is a continuous, progressive, and deepening work.

As we prepare now to work with a text of entrance meditation, let us review the steps that we shall follow.

We begin by sitting in stillness, then breathing in a regular rhythm. Working with the meditation texts, we close our eyes. We let ourselves be drawn into the twilight range of perception. Having gained entry there, we observe everything that presents itself to us. We make no judgments, neither accepting nor rejecting, but we take cognizance of whatever is present. We observe it all, and we record as much as we can in our Meditation Log. As we gather it together, the accumulation of data gradually discloses a direction and a purpose as new thoughts and images take form. We begin to see potentials of truth and new meaning unfolding through our inner experiences. We realize that it is not by directing nor by manipulating ourselves psychologically, but by being open in a disciplined way to the progressive stirrings within ourselves that we come personally into contact with the spiritual nature that is our individual and collective heritage as human beings.

Having said this much, we must understand that meditation in all its phases is a work that demonstrates itself and proves itself only as we actually do it. Therefore let us begin, sitting in stillness. . . .

> Letting the Self become still,
> Letting the breath become slow,
> Letting our thoughts come to rest.

THE
WELL
AND
THE
CATHEDRAL

I

Muddy / Clear:
The Mirror of the Water

Meditation Log *Date*

1. I remember the saying
    Of the old wise man, Lao Tse:
        "Muddy water,
        Let stand
        Becomes clear."

2. Thinking of that,
    I look within myself.
    I see,
    On the screen of my mind's eye,
    A stream of water,
    Moving,
    Swirling,
    Murky,
    It is full of things.
    I cannot look into this water.
    I cannot see my reflection
    In this water.

3. Now the movement stops.
   The water is in one place.
   It is heavy colored,
   Muddy
   But it is becoming quiet,
   The water is at rest.
   In its stillness
   The muddiness
   Is settling to the bottom.

4. At the surface it becomes clear,
   Transparent.
   I can see into the water
   More and more.
   Now I can see through
   To the very depth of it.
   There it shines
   And it reflects.

Meditation Log   *Date*

---

5. The heavens are reflected
   In the quiet water.
   It is clear.
   I see the reflection of a tree
   In the quiet water.
   The muddy water
   Has become clear.

6. As I continue to look
   Into the stillness
   A reflection of myself
   Begins to appear.
   Deep in the quietness
   Of the water,
   I see
   A reflection of myself,
   Myself
   In many different forms.

Meditation Log   *Date*

7.   I sit
In the stillness
And let the image shape itself.
It becomes many things.
Many images
Appear in the still water,
Many things
Come up for me to see.

8.   In the depth of the water,
The images
That open the greatest vision
Within me
Are not those that are visible.
I do not see them;
I just know them.
Something within me
Recognizes them
In the still water.

9. The muddy water has become quiet.
   I sit gazing into it,
   Seeing images,
   Visible and invisible,
   Letting them take form,
   Letting them change
   And re-form themselves
   In the depth of the still water,
   In the mirror of the water,
   In the depth of my Self,
   Moving, moving,
   In the Silence ... In the Silence.

II

Feeling the Movement
of Life

Meditation Log   Date

1. We go further,
    Exploring the deep places,
    Exploring what is not known to us,
    Exploring the open possibilities
    Of our life.

2. We have become quiet.
    We have looked
    Into the stillness of the waters.
    Having entered that stillness,
    We have learned
    That emptiness refills itself.
    Emptiness refills itself
    To overflowing
    With new ideas,
    Awarenesses,
    Relationships,
    As life renews itself
    Out of itself.

3. Knowing that, we relax.
   Emptiness refills itself.
   We let go,
   Breathing slowly,
   Letting go,
   Letting go of thoughts
   As they move within us.
   Each line of thought is free
   To unfold in its own way.
   Our thoughts being free,
   We are free of them.
   Our minds are quiet
   As we are quiet.

4. Our inner muscles,
   The muscles of the spirit,
   Are loose now,
   Loose and limber,
   Limber within ourselves,
   Free and able to move
   At the inward parts
   Of our Self.

5. We begin exploring
   In the stillness,
   Eyes closed,
   Feeling the movement of life,
   Our own life
   With its many phases,
   Cycles and changes,
   The changing movement of life,
   Our own life,
   The changing life of everyone.

6. Feeling the movement of life
   In all things
   And in everyone,
   Finding in the quiet water
   The elusive thread of life,
   Our life
   And the life of everyone,
   Retrieving the hidden thread
   Of meaning and direction
   In the movement of our life.

Meditation Log   *Date*

7. Exploring the deep places,
   Reaching inward
   To the memories and mysteries
   Of our life,
   Personal memories,
   And mysteries
   Much more than personal.

8. Restoring to ourselves
   The events of earlier years,
   Dreams fulfilled
   And unfulfilled,
   Plans and pains and laughter,
   Retracing
   The unremembered movements
   Of our life,
   Retrieving lost directions
   And forgotten goals.

Meditation Log

Date

---

9. Times that have been lost to us
    Return
    And become present
    As we seek them
    In the quiet waters.
    Events old and new
    Fit together
    As we look within,
    Finding the path of our life
    Finding the path of our life.

10. Eyes closed in stillness
    Breathing comes slow
    And deep.
    Breathing
    Inward, outward,
    Slowly.
    The waters within us
    Settle
    And become clear,
    Reflecting
    From the deep places.

11.   Images taking shape
      In the stillness of the water,
      Forming,
      Changing,
      Re-forming,
      Reflections of our life,
      Events old and new
      Revealed in them.
      Imagery of our life,
      Events old and new
      And things still to come,
      Reflecting the path of our life,
      Reflecting the path of our life
      In the Silence . . . In the Silence.

III

The Center Point
Within Me

Meditation Log

Date

1. We are resting,
   Physically quiet,
   Breath and body
   In gentle harmony
   Holding the stillness within.

2. Holding the stillness within,
   Thoughts fit into place.
   No longer spinning,
   They come together;
   No longer disputing,
   Our thoughts
   Are friendly with each other.
   The quality of wholeness
   Replaces
   The discord of the mind.

Meditation Log *Date*

3.   Mind and body
     Together,
     Thoughts and emotions
     Revolving around
     A single center point.
     Varied movements
     Actively churning
     Form a quiet center.
     A quiet center forms
     In their midst.

4.   We feel the center of our Self,
     The inner center of our Self,
     It is neither body
     Nor mind
     But a center point.
     Not this, not that,
     A single center point,
     The inner center of the Self.

Meditation Log   *Date*

5.   In the midst of activity
     Soft, slow breathing
     Sets a balance.
     An inward stillness
     Becomes present.
     The center point within me
     Establishes itself.

6.   For each of us it is so.
     A center point within
     Forms itself.
     A center point is present
     Not in space
     But in our being.

7.   A center point within me.
     My whole attention
     At that center point,
     Present there in the stillness,
     In the stillness of the Self.

8. Through this center point
    We move inward,
    Inward and downward
    Through a single straight shaft.
    It is as though we go
    Deep into the earth,
    But within our Self.
    Through the center point within
    We go inward,
    Deeper,
    Deeper inward.

9. My life
    Is like the shaft of a well.
    I go deep into it.
    The life of each of us
    Is a well.
    Its sources are deep,
    But it gives water on the surface.
    Now we go inward,
    Moving through our center point,
    Through our center point,
    Deeply inward to explore
    The infinities of our well.

Meditation Log _____ Date

10.   Long enough
        We have been on the surface
        Of our life.
        Now we go inward,
        Moving through our center point
        Inward,
        Into the well of our Self,
        Deeply,
        Further inward
        Into the well of our Self.

11.   We move away
        From the surface of things;
        We leave
        The circles of our thoughts,
        Our habits, customs.
        All the shoulds
        And the oughts
        Of our life
        We leave behind.

12. We leave them on the surface
    While we go inward,
    Into the depth of our life
    Moving through the center point
    Into the well of our Self
    As deeply
    As fully
    As freely as we can.
    Through the center point
    Exploring the deep places.
    Exploring the deep places
    In the Silence ... In the Silence.

IV

*Into the Well of
the Self*

Meditation Log   *Date*

1. Eyes closed
   We move inward
   Through our center point,
   Deeper,
   Further inward
   Into the well of the Self,
   Exploring
   In the silence there,
   In the darkness there.

2. We move in the darkness
   Trying to see.
   The silent darkness
   Is like muddy water
   Within our Self
   Until it settles,
   Until it clears.
   Then the darkness becomes light.
   It shines.
   The light shines in the darkness,
   In the darkness
   Of the Self

Meditation Log   *Date*

3. Waiting with eyes closed,
   Now we are able to see.
   Here in the midst of the darkness,
   The silence resonates
   And begins to speak to us.
   Here in the darkness,
   Here in the silence
   Of the well of our life,
   We begin to see
   And we begin to hear.

4. We move about
   Exploring,
   Observing,
   And recording
   All that we discover
   In the depths
   Of the well of our life.
   We each go down our own well,
   The well of our life.
   We do not go down another's well
   But only our own,
   Sometimes sending images
   From the deep places
   As messages
   To those around us.

5. We move about with freedom
   In the depths
   Of the well of our life.
   We explore privately
   And yet together,
   Exploring the fullness of our life,
   Its joys and sadness,
   Letting our life
   Reflect itself to us
   In forms old and new.

6. Exploring the deep places
   Our life returns to us.
   Outward experiences
   And inward experiences,
   We taste them again
   And know them as they are
   Without judging them,
   Without being angry or resentful,
   Without being proud,
   Without being ashamed,
   But knowing
   The experiences of our life
   As they have been
   And as they are.

7. Eyes closed
    We are moving inward
    Into the well of our life,
    Into the well of our Self,
    Taking note of what we see
    And what we hear,
    Of what we smell
    And taste and feel,
    Exploring the depth of our life.

8. Exploring the depth of our life,
    Observing and recording,
    We recognize
    The many dimensions
    Of the outer/inner universe
    As they are reflected in us,
    In the silent darkness,
    In the well of our Self.

9.   Reflections of our life,
     Reflections of our Self,
     Personal
     And more than personal,
     Present themselves to us
     Whether we see or hear them.
     These reflections are the *images*
     That reveal to us
     The inner quality of our being,
     The inner quality of our life.

10. We direct our attention now
     To beholding them.
     We behold them inwardly
     With every sensitivity we possess,
     With every form of sensing,
     Of seeing, hearing,
     Smelling, touching, feeling,
     And especially
     Directly knowing.
     Directly knowing
     We behold inwardly.

11.   Every mode of awareness
       Inwardly alert,
       Inwardly perceptive,
       Beholding everywhere
       And everything
       As we move about
       In the well of our Self,
       Exploring,
       Observing,
       Recording,
       In the Silence ... In the Silence.

V

The Downward/Upward

Journey

Meditation Log   *Date*

1. We continue.
   We have moved away from the surface.
   We have gone into our life
   To discover and explore
   The depth of our well.

2. In the quiet
   Focusing inward,
   Our breath moves slowly,
   Deeply,
   Inward, outward.
   The breath moves at the center,
   At the center point within;
   The breath moves at the center,
   At the center of the Self.

3. We direct our minds
   To this center point
   At the inward depth
   Of our Self.
   Our attention is focused there,
   We are present there
   Within our Self.

4.   The center point relaxes.
It loosens,
Stretches, opens.
The center point
Becomes the shaft of the well
Within our Self.
It is opening wider;
Its walls are softening,
The shaft within us is opening,
Making space so we can move
Further down the well
Into the depth of our Self.

5.   We go inward,
Inward.
We go deeper,
Deeper.
We go further away
And ever closer to our Self.
We move more easily now.
Being less fearful
Of what is strange to us,
We move more naturally,
Letting ourselves be drawn
Deeper inward.

6.   As we move further
Into the darkness,
Into the silence,
We find that the light is ample,
More than ample.
Much is shown to us
In varied phases.

7.   Many shapes and forms,
Sounds and smells,
Many visions and symbols
Present themselves
To the inward eye.
It is an inward knowing,
A direct knowing.
A beholding
Through our life
Of dimensions beyond our life.

8.   Much that we never perceived before
Is presenting itself to us now.
As these perceptions come to us,
We record them.
We write them as we perceive them.
We go inward to behold them
And we come upward
Briefly, quickly
To record what has been shown to us
At the depth of the well.

9.   We record
So that we shall remember
The atmosphere
And the reality we have known.
In time to come
We shall consider
And reconsider
The multiple messages
That were given to us
At the depth of the well.

10. We go downward
    Slowly and deeply.
    We come upward
    Quickly and briefly
    To write what needs to be recorded,
    Then to return
    To the depth of the well.

11. Again and again
    We complete the cycle
    Of our downward/upward journey.
    Each time
    A little further downward
    And then up;
    Each time
    A little further inward
    And then out;
    Each time a little further
    From the surface of our life
    Moving toward the depth
    Of the well,
    Moving toward the source
    Beyond the well
    A little at a time.

12. We continue
    Our downward/upward journey,
    Our inward/outward journey.
    Beholding inwardly
    We recognize in the darkness
    What cannot be seen
    In the light,
    Recognizing,
    Recording,
    Exploring the deep places
    On our downward/upward journey
    In the Silence ... In the Silence

VI

*The Waters
Beyond the Well*

1. We have been going downward
   And then upward,
   Inward and then outward.
   Each time as we go deeper
   The atmosphere softens to us.
   It becomes more comfortable,
   More congenial.
   It absorbs us more warmly.
   We know
   We belong here.

2. The deeper we go,
   The further
   We move from our daily life,
   The further
   From our accustomed ways.
   We see strange things
   But they are not strange to us.

Meditation Log

Date

3. Something in our Self
   Recognizes
   These new perceptions.
   The further downward we go,
   The further inward we go,
   The more we recognize
   That we are coming home,
   Coming home to our Self.

4. It is good being home,
   Being at home in our Self.
   We can do many things
   Being at home in our Self.
   Moving inward and outward,
   Feeling stronger now
   Than when we began.

5. We move inward again
    Deeper than before.
    We perceive something beyond us,
    Beyond the furthest depth
    Of our well.
    It seems to be the source
    Of our well.
    It is drawing us toward it,
    Drawing us into it.
    We willingly go,
    Letting ourselves be drawn there.

6. We go downward and inward
    Freely
    Letting ourselves be drawn
    Through the silent darkness.
    We have passed through
    The full depth of the well.
    Beyond the well
    There is a stream.
    At last we have come
    To the underground stream.

7.   All at once
     We are within the underground stream.
     We did not need to enter it.
     It drew us to it.
     It drew us into it.
     We are moving freely
     Within it now.

8.   We are exploring
     In the underground stream.
     Its waters are pleasant.
     They flow gently around us
     And they are buoyant.
     They sustain us.
     They support and carry us.
     The stream is deep
     But its waters are buoyant.
     So none can be lost
     In the underground stream.

Meditation Log   *Date*

9.   We are exploring together
     In the underground stream.
     Each of us came down our own well
     Alone
     As a private person,
     But we are all meeting here
     In the underground stream.

10. All our separate wells
     Lead to this underground stream.
     It is the deep resource
     For all of us.
     All our wells draw from it.
     It is our source of supply.
     These moving waters
     Are home for each of us.

Meditation Log   *Date*

11.   There are no separations here.
       We intermingle freely.
       We find that we *know* things,
       We see visions,
       We hear sounds,
       We have perceptions,
       Recognitions,
       Intuitions of truths
       That were mysterious to us before
       But here
       In the underground stream
       We know them directly.

12.   They come to us as symbols,
       But the symbols open to us
       Like the bud of a flower
       And we look into them
       Deeply,
       Infinitely inward.
       The bud opens level after level.
       We look
       Into the depth of the flower,
       Into the depth of the symbol,
       Deep, deep,
       As deep as the heart can see.

Meditation Log   *Date*

13. Everything we behold
    We draw into our Self.
    As we were drawn into the stream
    So we draw it into our Self.
    The underground stream
    Is one with us,
    As we are one
    With the underground stream.
    It flows around us
    And it flows within us.
    We share
    The unity of Being.
    We share
    The unity of Being
    In the Silence ... In the Silence.

VII

Sharing The
Underground Stream

Meditation Log   *Date*

1. We have made the journey
    Into the well of our Self
    And beyond our Self
    Into the moving waters
    Of the underground stream.
    Downward/upward,
    Inward again,
    We are here
    In the waters beyond the well.

2. Many awarenesses
    Have been given to us
    In the waters beyond the well.
    Symbols have opened to us,
    Riddles of life,
    Visions of things to come;
    The struggles and harmonies
    In the movement of the universe
    Have disclosed themselves to us
    One by one.

Meditation Log   *Date*

3.   Here in the underground stream
     We realize
     That many others
     In earlier times
     Have entered their wells
     And have gone inward
     Until they reached
     The waters beyond the well
     Where we are now.

4.   In ancient days
     Jacob went down his well,
     And where he returned
     He placed a stone
     For remembrance.
     In his way, Moses went down,
     And Isaiah and Ezekiel,
     Lao Tse and Zoroaster,
     Gotama Siddhartha,
     Jesus of Nazareth,
     Teresa and Juliana,
     Meister Eckhart,
     George Fox,
     Waldo Emerson and Walt Whitman,
     And many others
     Have gone down their well
     To the underground stream.

5.   These and many more have been here,
Some famous in history,
Others unknown,
But each by direct beholding
Discovered
Many marvelous things
That were shown to them
Or that they recognized
And drew to themselves
In the underground stream.

6.   Those who have gone down their well
Into the underground stream
Have done many things
Upon returning
To the surface of their lives.
Some have written books,
Some have painted and sculpted,
Some have made philosophies,
Some have stated doctrines,
Some have lived their lives
More fully
With inward abundance
And with gentler wisdom
Than was possible before.

Meditation Log   *Date*

7. We think of them,
   Those who have been here before us,
   As we ourselves
   Enter the underground stream.
   We are not the first
   Nor shall we be the last
   To go
   Through the center point of Self
   Into the well
   And beyond the well
   Into the underground stream.

8. Now we have entered the stream,
   Ourselves
   And more than ourselves,
   Present to one another
   Beyond separateness
   In the unity of Being,
   Accessible to everyone,
   Sharing with all
   In the unity of Being.

9.   Sharing the underground stream
      We recognize others here,
      Not only we who are entering now
      But those who have been here before us.
      Their quality of being,
      Their atmosphere,
      Still is present
      In the underground stream.

10.   Those who have been here before us
      Century upon century
      Have left the imprint of their presence
      On the waters
      Of the underground stream.
      Through the quality of their being
      They will speak with us.
      They will share with us
      Their atmosphere
      And their awareness,
      Their lives and their knowledge,
      The quality of their being
      In the timeless unity.
      In the timeless unity
      They will share with us
      As one.

Meditation Log　　　　　　　　　　　*Date*

11. Sharing the underground stream
    We are invited to speak,
    To ask our questions,
    To consider the answers
    And to record what is said.
    We are invited to speak,
    To share in dialogue
    Here in the underground stream,
    Listening and speaking
    With those who have entered before us
    And have left their mark
    Upon the atmosphere
    Of the underground stream.
    Their quality of being
    Is awaiting us
    In the timeless waters.

Meditation Log   *Date*

12. Gratefully
    We greet them,
    Speaking and listening,
    Our hearts open to their wisdom,
    Asking and hearing,
    Speaking of all life,
    Speaking of our life,
    With those who have been here before us.
    Their quality of being is present,
    Present for us now.
    We are speaking and listening
    In the Silence . . . In the Silence.

VIII

Entering the
Cathedral

1. Much we have learned
    In the underground stream,
    Some that was shown to us,
    Some that was spoken to us.
    We draw it all into our Self
    As we were drawn
    Into the underground stream.
    We shall continue to absorb it
    And learn from it
    Now that we know how to reach
    And enter
    The underground stream.

2. Those who have been there before us
    Have much to teach us
    Of what they learned there
    And what took place
    When they returned
    From the underground stream.

3.   Where they came back,
       Where they emerged from the well,
       Many placed a stone for remembrance
       As Jacob had done.
       And many others,
       Who did not themselves
       Reach the depth of the stream,
       Also placed a stone
       To commemorate
       The remarkable event
       Of which they had heard.

4.   Each placed a stone
       As a token
       And many placed their stones
       Together,
       One building upon the other,
       Until soon
       A magnificent cathedral
       Covered the well,
       The well that led
       To the underground stream.

5. Since that time
   Many have come to the cathedral
   To pay their respects,
   To praise the name of their God,
   To ask favors of many kinds.
   They all seem to know
   That something important is there,
   That something important is present
   At the site of the cathedral.

6. The well
   That leads to the underground stream
   Is at the base of the cathedral.
   But now it is covered by stones
   And difficult to find.

7. How shall we get to the well
   Now that it has been covered
   By the stones of the cathedral,
   Now that it has been hidden
   By the passage
   Of the centuries?

8.　We have found a way.
　　We can go there together.
　　There is a shaft of a well
　　Beneath the cathedral.
　　And where is the cathedral?
　　We have nowhere to look
　　And nowhere to go,
　　For you are the cathedral,
　　I am the cathedral.
　　The way to the underground stream
　　Is the well
　　That is hidden within us.

9.　Wherever we are
　　Our cathedral is present;
　　When we seek a quiet place
　　In the midst of turmoil,
　　A refuge
　　From the pressures of the world,
　　Wherever we are,
　　Whatever is happening
　　Our cathedral is present
　　And open for us.

10. Entering the cathedral
    Is sanctuary
    From the hurricanes of life,
    A quiet center
    Wherever we are,
    Whatever is happening.

11. Entering the cathedral
    We become still;
    Our eyes closed,
    We breathe slowly,
    Inward, outward,
    Feeling the center of our body,
    Feeling the center of our Self,
    Feeling the center point within.

Meditation Log   *Date*

12. Entering the cathedral
    We focus inward,
    Directing ourselves
    Through the center point within.
    The muddy waters of our life
    Become tranquil and clear,
    They become a mirror
    Reflecting within us
    The depths and heights of being.
    Thus the way inward
    Opens to us.
    We find the well
    Beneath the cathedral.

13. Entering the cathedral
     Wherever we may be,
     The center point within us
     Becomes the well
     That opens inward.
     We move into that well
     And beyond it
     Into the buoyant waters
     Of the underground stream
     Where we are now . . .
     Joining those
     Who have been here before us
     In the timeless unity,
     In the timeless unity
     Where we are now
     In the Silence . . . In the Silence.

PERSPECTIVES

1. From the Anonymous Monk to the Modern Person

We have seen that our work with *The Well and the Cathedral* proceeds step by step, level by level, cycle by cycle. As one unit of meditation is completed, another is set into motion. Each feeds into and becomes the starting point for the next, so that our spiritual work builds a chain of experiences reaching depths, touching peaks, progressively expanding the range of our awareness and refining the quality of our being.

When we consider the continuity of our experience over a period of time, we realize that our inner quest proceeds as though it has a life of its own. It is drawn forward by a guidance that unfolds from within us, moving in directions and making discoveries that could not have been anticipated when the work began. Without understanding the reasons, we find ourselves being led to our next steps, often in the midst of confusion and disappointment, and sometimes despair. Even those beliefs and actions that might be regarded as errors eventually become teachers to us as we continue on our quest.

In a profound sense there is no such thing as making mistakes on the spiritual dimension of life. All our experiences feed into a single inner process that self-adjusts as it proceeds. At each point it establishes a new balance in which the contents of our life are each given a place and a value that is appropriate to that moment. As we add new experiences, whether they satisfy or disturb us, they bring about a readjustment to a new condition of balance, and thus take us an additional step along our way.

Each of us, a unique individual in the universe, is striving to connect with a truth that is valid for everyone. We are reaching toward universals of meaning, but since we can see our truths only through the coloration of our life experience, we call them by many different names. What is more important, it is a truth that presents itself in many degrees. We may have some degree of it but not all of it, just as we may eat some of the fruit on a tree but not all.

There are many models in history of persons who built their lives spiritually by degrees, proceeding a step at a time. One of these was the fourteenth century monk who wrote *The Cloud of Unknowing*. While preparing this edition of *The Well and the Cathedral* I have found myself thinking back to 1956 when I transposed that text into modern English, mainly to help myself follow the subtleties of the anonymous monk so that I could undertake his meditations.

At that time I recommended the monk's approach partly because of his earthy, realistic, humorous, no-nonsense style of dealing with the delicate phenomena of the inner life; partly because of the breadth of perspective that enabled him to see beyond the boundaries of the medieval world to the universals of spirit; and especially because of the experimental attitude he brought to the entire realm of spiritual involvement. As a spiritual pragmatist, the monk of *The Cloud of Unknowing* followed the same trial-and-error approach that a modern empiricist uses in a laboratory. But he applied it to the life of the spirit.

The goal of the monk was to experience connection with the great Unity of Being, which he called God and referred to in the medieval language of churchly observance. But he approached his goal in a way that has much in common with the spirit of modern science. Nonetheless, when I called the monk's work to the attention of the public at that time there was very little response. In those days there were relatively few in western civilization who acknowledged the value of working actively in the processes of the inner life. The prevailing tone of the culture was extroverted and rationalistic, and people appreciated the importance only of hard tangible facts. To speak of being empirical and experimental with respect to the elusive intangibles of the inner life seemed to be a contradiction in terms.

Attitudes have changed since then, however, and the last decade especially has brought a greater appreciation of the vision of the anonymous monk as well as similar historical efforts. Nowadays when I speak of his experimental approach to spiritual experience, it receives a much friendlier response.

However, there is a major difficulty that still prevents the modern person from becoming involved in the monk's program: the medieval Christian symbolism which the monk used as the vehicle for his profound spiritual contact is now for cultural reasons an obstacle to many persons. Rather than serving as a vehicle for them, it is a barrier between their inner selves and the unitary connective experience. And yet, as my contact with large numbers of persons has increased during the past years, it has become clear to me that many are seeking essentially the same experience of unity that the monk was describing. But to the twentieth century ear, the monk's cultural tone and the historical symbols in which he expressed his experiences have an alien sound. Because the language belongs to an earlier, now foreign, and largely rejected time of history, the words can be heard but not the meaning behind them.

This barrier to the message of the monk of *The Cloud of Unknowing* also prevents many persons from recognizing the validity of other paths to spiritual connection described by historical figures who reached the unitary experience. When the spiritual teachers of earlier times set out to convey the particular truth they had found, or to teach the steps by which they came to it, they could do so only in terms of the symbols and images that had been the carriers of their experience. And yet the life of each had a specific dateline in history. Each came from a particular culture that left its characteristic imprint upon it. And each bore the marks of the subjective depths, the private encounter with the ultimates of existence, that distinguished their unique experience. These particularities are their trademark, like the monk's medieval symbolism in *The Cloud of Unknowing*. Sometimes the symbols open a road that enables others to share the experience of spiritual teachers in history. But very often the symbols become barriers that separate us from the original unitary contact that they brought about.

In the course of my own searchings, I have had the occasion to know both of these experiences. Sometimes I have been able to share the inner contact of the great teachers by entering the symbols that were their vehicles. At other times their symbols have become barriers to me because I was unable to penetrate their exterior.

Eventually I learned that whenever I was able to move inward deeply enough, I could participate to some degree in the connective experience they had achieved. At those times it was as though I swam underwater beneath the blockages presented by their particular symbols and doctrines so that I was able to reach the core of their experience. Thus their inner wisdom became accessible without the impediments of their outer trappings.

This way of interior connection has helped me penetrate the surface of the teachings and disciplines that I have explored over the years: zen, contemplative Christianity, Hasidism, various cosmic philosophers and poets, Lao Tse, Sufism, and especially the prophetic spirit of the Old Testament. The influence of each of these teachings as well as of others, is to be found in the text of *The Well and the Cathedral*, although the symbolism of none is expressed directly.

Something more important, however, than their symbolism is very strongly present. It is the underlying process by which each achieved a unitary connection that gave an energy and a meaning to their lives. As we work toward this in our modern situation, the question of what such a unitary connection involves becomes of great significance, especially in relation to our experience with *The Well and the Cathedral*.

In the introductory sentence he placed at the head of his book, the monk says, "This is a book of contemplation called *The Cloud of Unknowing* in which a soul is united with God." In the original version, the medieval phrase he used was "oned with God" and the additional overtones there clarify the experience. "Unitary connection" means to be united in the sense of "being made one with" a reality that is other than and larger than oneself. But in the moment when we become one with it, it no longer is an "other" to us, and we are no longer an "other" to it. We have become united with it, connected in such a way that there is no separation between us.

This unity of being is sometimes spoken of as love. It is not love in the sense of a feeling of affection, but love in the profound Biblical sense of "knowing" in both actual and symbolic terms. As when Adam "knew" Eve, it was an act of oneness in which opposites were connected in unity.

The experience of oneness encompasses and overcomes the separateness of human existence. It transcends the conflicts and competitiveness of society, and to that degree it opens a way to human transformation. But what does the experience of unity actually involve?

Individuals perceive and describe it variously. For some it is a union with the universe, a melting away of the person in a suffusion of cosmic wholeness. This is what Freud referred to as the "oceanic feeling." He said he respected those who reported having had such experiences, but that he was temperamentally unable to understand what they were describing.

For others, Unity of Being is a more specific

connective experience, as when the monk speaks of seeking oneness between God and the soul. We have to interpret that in terms of the symbolic framework of his mind and the context of his culture. To the monk, God is the one reality that has meaning in the universe. Indeed, to the monk God *is* meaning; and everything else is relative to that reality.

When the monk speaks of the "soul," it has more than one aspect. On one level, he means by the soul the specific individual entity that is the object of salvation within the worldview of Christianity. The full spiritual discipline he sets forth in his treatise, however, indicates that his understanding of the "soul" has an additional and more encompassing scope. To him the soul is the whole interior realm within which the struggles and the strivings of the spirit are experienced. It is the space within us where the work of reaching toward unity with God is to be carried through. It contains the resources, the energies, the qualities, and the "stirrings," like the "image of God" within, that supply us and enable us to pursue the goal of unity.

The monk's larger understanding of the soul gives us a clue as to how the experience of unitary connection can be approached in the modern world. His narrower, more specific view of the soul is limited to those who share in his traditional concept and hold it as an article of faith. On the other hand, his larger view of the soul, as the universe within ourselves where spiritual work is carried through, provides a perspective in which all of us can seek the unitary experience. The first concept is one that is bounded by a particular culture and tradition. While it does afford an experience of connection, it can do so only within its own terms. But the larger view of the soul gives us a range that reaches beyond special beliefs. It gives us a perspective in which the experience of unitary connection between the outer cosmic universe and the inner universe of the self can be appreciated without being limited by particular cultural/historical symbols or beliefs.

Over the years these reflections on the anonymous monk of *The Cloud of Unknowing* have sharpened for me the distinction between the outer forms in which spiritual experiences take place and the inner process by means of which they unfold. Interestingly enough, it is the outer forms of traditional faith that are breaking down in modern times and that breakdown has highly significant effects. It throws people back upon themselves and forces them to pay attention to the validity of the experiences that occur within the depth of their own inner universe.

For many of us, to be thrown back upon ourselves becomes a frightening, almost nightmarish experience. We feel there are no resources for us to draw upon and we fall into the anxiety state which the existentialist phraseology describes as the "dread" at finding "no exit" from the dilemmas of existence. Psychiatry, looking at the same situation, sees it meriting a diagnosis of neurosis. But our experience with *The Well and the Cathedral* opens another possibility. It takes us on a narrow pathway inward that eludes existential dread on the one side and medical diagnosis on the other while it carries us to the depths of our being.

2. The Unitary Connection

When the historical traditions lose their power to guide us, we are turned back to the resources of our own individuality. There we experience our all-too-human limitations and the feelings of anxiety that are inherent in being a finite person in an infinite universe. As we proceed into the depths of the Self, however, we come to a place that is beyond dread and diagnosis, beyond both the darkness of existentialism and the pathology of medicine. It is an inward place, and we reach it when we have gone far enough into the well of our Self to enter the underground stream.

Numerous new awarenesses come to us here and they have a renewing effect. Many of the conditions that psychiatry has interpreted as illnesses are healed here. The reason for this is primarily that contact with the underground stream gives a light of meaning for the existential darkness. We realize, then, that as we move inward through the well of Self, we are taking steps toward wholeness as we are deepening the relationship between our individuality and the universe.

The underground stream is a place of unity where experiences of personal and cosmic wholeness are brought about. Considered as a symbol or as a teaching, the underground stream is altogether neutral and altogether accepting. It rejects none but it has room for every type of doctrine. In the underground stream beliefs that seem to be in opposition can come together and draw each other toward wholeness. At that deep level the fluid sense of time makes room for change and incorporates it into the process of spiritual growth. Differences in philosophy that sometimes seem to be in sharp contradiction to one another are absorbed into the continuation of history. By means of their conflict, the unitary connections of life are being reinforced and made more profound.

When we speak of the underground stream, we recognize it to be the same as the place to which the monk of *The Cloud of Unknowing* was referring when he spoke of "The ground of naked being." It is the place where "oneness with God" may be known as a reality and where we can experience unitary connection with life. Since it is a place that can be described by many different names, it is beyond the phraseology of any particular religion. Yet it enables us to recognize the core of truth in many religions.

A primary contribution of the anonymous monk lies in the concept and method he provided for working toward unitary experience. His limitation and his unavailability for the modern mind comes from the fact that the symbolic forms in which he presented his program necessarily reflected the attitudes and beliefs of his time. Modern persons who are not in tune with those medieval constructs necessarily find it difficult to follow the monk's instructions even though they are intuitively in accord with his goals. There is, however, a way of interior practice that corresponds to the process the monk recommended for achieving a unifying contact with the ground of Being. Using a neutral set of symbols as their vehicle, the sequence of meditations with which we have just worked in *The Well and the Cathedral* serve as a modern equivalent to the procedures of *The Cloud of Unknowing*.

The essence of his format and method is contained in his view of the soul as a large interior area in which the practical work of unitary experience can be carried through. Step by step he moves into the depths of the inner space of the soul until the atmosphere in which he finds himself is markedly different from his accustomed condition of rational consciousness. It is a "Cloud of Unknowing" which not only is placed between him and his God but also serves as the deep ground of meeting where the unitary connection can be established as an abiding quality of his personal being.

The monk's ultimate goal is to achieve unity with God. Toward this, he describes as his core spiritual process a series of interior cycles through which one must pass again and again. The eight units of experience in *The Well and the Cathedral* traverse an inward path that parallels this as it follows its principle of progressive deepening through a full cycle of meditation. It does this, however, in a context of symbolism that is more accessible to the modern mind not only because it is neutral with respect to religious doctrine, but because of its universality in the larger perspective of history. The symbol of the well, for example, has appeared in spiritual writings since the most ancient days as a representation of the path of spiritual connection. So pervasive has its use in this way been over the centuries that the symbolic associations it evokes are now virtually self evident. As a modern metaphor it enables us to move toward unitary contact in neutral terms that fulfill a religious function while they are also in accord with our psychological understanding.

The symbol of the well implies individuality, insofar as each well is separate from every other well, just as each life is separate from every other life. As we descend into the well of Self, therefore, we move through levels of experience that reflect our personal existence. Personal memory is the first of these. We recall the events of our life.

> "Exploring the deep places,
> Our life returns to us."

Moving deeper, we come to a level of memory that is much more than personal. It is the memory of history, of experiences that belong not to ourselves

alone but to the memory of humankind. Awarenesses come to us that are derived from events we
have not experienced personally, but which in some
mysterious way have left their traces in our consciousness.

> "Personal memories,
> And mysteries
> Much more than personal."

We find ourselves being brought into touch with
circumstances and beliefs that express the encounter
with reality not of ourselves but of the lives of other
persons in other times and places. As we move
further into the depths of our well, we are given
glimpses of events that pertain to others in our
genealogy, in our historical line of inheritance, and
others in our cultural or religious tradition. Sometimes we are given awareness of events that are far
removed from our particular path in history, drawn
from cultures and traditions that are foreign to us.
They may seem to be foreign, but they are not alien
to us. When we are given glimpses of them as we
move through our well, an understanding of the
larger dimensions of their meaning also comes to us.

We find that we have cognitions of symbolic
and other mysteries of life greater than any knowledge we had learned or been taught on the outer
level of our experience. As we move down into our
well, we find that we are able to know things that
we did not think we knew. Knowledge comes to us

beyond our individual experiences. History speaks to us on many levels, depending on the sensitivity to it that our practice has given us. We gain a greater understanding of events that relate to our individual life, and also an intuitive awareness of the universals of human experience. The deeper we go into our well, the further we move beyond the subjectivities of our individual life and the more directly we touch fundamental truths of existence.

The metaphor of the well represents the individuality and uniqueness of our life, but the further we go into it the more completely we transcend the separateness of our ego-existence. It expresses the profound paradox that the more we move inward into our privacy and individuality, the more we become connected to the wholeness and richness of the universe. At its deeper levels we experience an expansion of consciousness that enables us to feel we are not limited to being only ourselves. We move through the well of the Self into a dimension beyond it, and that is when we come to the underground stream. Here we experience the Unity of Being and are one with it. It is the place of transcendence where, after a long inward journey, self-transformation and renewal begin.

About the Author

Dr. Ira Progoff is the creator of the widely accepted *Intensive Journal* method of personal development and its related approach of Process Meditation. He is the author of numerous books. *At a Journal Workshop* (1975) and *The Practice of Process Meditation* (1980) are the two textbooks that describe the ways of using the *Intensive Journal* techniques. In *Life-Study* (1983) the *Intensive Journal* method is extended to provide a means of re-experiencing creative lives from history.

The conceptual base of Ira Progoff's work is contained in a trilogy of books. *The Death and Rebirth of Psychology* (1956) crystallizes the cumulative results of the work of Freud, Adler, Jung and Rank to build the foundation for a new psychology of personal growth. *Depth Psychology and Modern Man* (1959) presents the evolutionary and philosophical perspectives, and formulates basic concepts which make creative experience possible. *The Symbolic and the Real* (1963) pursues the practical and religious implications of these ideas.

The *Intensive Journal* method emerged in 1966 as a system of techniques for individuals to use in their personal growth. It has since become a national program that includes ecumenical retreats for religious experience not limited by doctrine.

Dr. Progoff's *Intensive Journal* method has been described in *Psychology Today* as a "unique tool . . . to help secularized Americans rediscover the spiritual."

Currently Dr. Progoff is Director of Dialogue House which, from its New York headquarters, conducts national workshop and training programs on the use of the *Intensive Journal* process in its various personal, social and spiritual applications.